LIGHTHOUSES
of the
WEST COAST
Washington, Oregon, and California

RAY JONES

Globe Pequot

Essex, Connecticut

Globe Pequot

An imprint of Globe Pequot, the trade division of
The Rowman & Littlefield Publishing Group, Inc.
4501 Forbes Blvd., Ste. 200
Lanham, MD 20706
www.rowman.com

Distributed by NATIONAL BOOK NETWORK

British Library Cataloguing in Publication Information available

Library of Congress Cataloging-in-Publication Data

Names: Jones, Ray, 1948– author.
Title: Lighthouses of the West Coast : Washington, Oregon, and California / Ray Jones.
Description: Essex CT : Globe Pequot, [2023] | Includes index.
Identifiers: LCCN 2022047930 (print) | LCCN 2022047931 (ebook) | ISBN 9781493047321 (paper) | ISBN 9781493047338 (epub)
Subjects: LCSH: Lighthouses—Pacific Coast (U.S.)—Guidebooks. | Lighthouses—California—Guidebooks. | Lighthouses—Oregon—Guidebooks. | Lighthouses—Washington (State)—Guidebooks.
Classification: LCC VK1024.P32 J66 2023 (print) | LCC VK1024.P32 (ebook) | DDC 387—dc23/eng/20221012
LC record available at https://lccn.loc.gov/2022047930
LC ebook record available at https://lccn.loc.gov/2022047931

♾️™ The paper used in this publication meets the minimum requirements of American National Standard for Information Sciences—Permanence of Paper for Printed Library Materials, ANSI/NISO Z39.48-1992.

Contents

PART TWO
ROMANTIC BEACONS OF THE EMERALD COAST: OREGON

PART THREE
ROMANTIC BEACONS OF THE REDWOOD CLIFFS: NORTHERN CALIFORNIA

PART FOUR
ROMANTIC BEACONS OF
THE GOLDEN SHORES:
CENTRAL AND SOUTHERN CALIFORNIA

California's Pigeon Point Light stands at the edge of the 5000-mile-wide Pacific.

Introduction

The West is where America reaches its outer limits, for here the continent comes to an abrupt and spectacular end. Here the "westward-ho" migrations of the pioneers were finally halted. They could go no farther, for the West Coast lies at the edge of an ocean more than 5,000 miles wide. So vast is the Pacific that it is larger by far than all the earth's landmasses combined.

The Pacific is so enormous and so stormy that throughout human history only the bravest mariners have challenged it. We will never know how many paid for their daring with their lives, but the number, if we knew it, would be impressive. No doubt, many simply vanished into the ocean's trackless, watery wastes. Many others came to grief at the margins of the Pacific, near where, at long last, it touches land. The American West Coast is one such place, and from the point of view of mariners, far more threatening than most for its shoreline stretches more than 2,000 rock-strewn miles, from Cape Flattery in the north to San Diego in the south.

Most maritime disasters happen not on the open sea but near the coast. For as long as ships have sailed the seas, sailors have paid with their lives when their vessels have come too close to the shore. Ships are built to withstand the stresses of high winds and giant waves, but a collision with rock, reef, or sand is usually fatal.

Unfortunately for many, such deadly encounters between ship and shore are common along the American West Coast. Stony capes jut out into the ocean like knife blades. Massive blocks of stone rise unexpectedly from the waves. Swift-running streams wash mud and gravel out of the mountains to form ship-killing shallows and block off the entrances of the rivers, where sea captains might otherwise find safe harbor from a storm.

Lighting the West

To help mariners navigate safely in the face of these dangers, the US Congress launched an ambitious construction program in the 1850s aimed at raising lighthouse towers at strategic locations along the West Coast. Lighthouses perform two key services: They help navigators keep their ships on course, and they warn of impending calamity. The latter is, of course, their most vital and dramatic function: saving ships and lives.

Government lighthouse officials hurried a survey team to the West in 1848. Its members painstakingly navigated the wild and dangerous western shores. On more than one occasion the survey ships themselves came near disaster for lack of adequate charts and shore lights to guide their helmsmen. But the surveyors persevered, approaching treacherous headlands, sizing up dangerous rocks, charting capes, noting likely construction sites, even meeting with local Native American chiefs to see if their tribes were hostile and likely to attack construction crews.

The survey team compiled a report recommending establishment of a string of lighthouses from Canada to Mexico. The report pointed to locations where the need for coastal markers was most critical—key harbors, important river entrances, threatening rocks and reefs. By 1852 Congress had narrowed the survey list to sixteen sites where construction of lighthouses was to begin immediately. Among those with congressional authorization were Cape Disappointment, Cape Flattery, New Dungeness, Smith Island, and Willapa Bay in Washington, the entrance to the Umpqua River in Oregon, Humboldt Harbor and Crescent City in northern California, Alcatraz Island, Fort Point, Point Bonita, and the Farallon Islands near San Francisco, and Point Loma, Santa Barbara, Point Pinos, and Point Conception along the southern California coast. Congress appropriated $148,000 to launch the project, an impressive sum at the time, but one that would prove woefully inadequate.

Trying to stretch these federal dollars as far as possible, government officials decided to hire a single contractor to build the first eight lights, seven of them in California and one in Oregon. Unfortunately, the savings that might have been realized through this approach never got beyond the door of the US Treasury. Through a corrupt paper-shuffling scheme, the contract was given to an unscrupulous Treasury Department official who understood nothing about the construction of lighthouses. He had no intention of building them himself and quickly sold the contract to a Baltimore firm, reaping a handsome profit in the process.

The company that ended up with the contract was a partnership of Francis Kelly and Francis Gibbons. The latter was a veteran lighthouse engineer who had built the Bodie Island Lighthouse on the Outer Banks of North Carolina. Kelly and Gibbons loaded up the sailing ship *Oriole* with supplies and sent it off to California by way of Cape Horn at the southern tip of South America.

When the *Oriole* arrived at San Francisco late in 1852, Gibbons's construction crew began work immediately on the Alcatraz Island Lighthouse. Gibbons believed he and his men could build several lighthouses at once and that the work could be done faster and more efficiently in stages. So once the foundation was finished on Alcatraz, he moved part of his crew to Fort Point, where they prepared the site and started laying a second foundation. Hopping from place to place in this way, Gibbons's workers had four lighthouses standing within ten months. Then disaster struck.

In August 1853 the *Oriole* set sail from San Francisco to the mouth of the Columbia River, where work was scheduled to begin on a fifth lighthouse at Cape Disappointment. Having no light to guide her, the ship struck shoals near the entrance of the river and began to take on water. Feverish efforts to save the vessel proved unsuccessful, and she sank, carrying all the remaining construction materials down with her. Fortunately, the ship's crew and its complement of lighthouse builders were rescued.

Gibbons and Kelly scrambled frantically to replace the lost materials. Within a few months the partners had commissioned another ship and stocked her with supplies so that work could resume. By redoubling their efforts, they were able to get the project back on schedule. In August 1854, one year after the sinking of the *Oriole*, the last brick was laid on the Point Loma Lighthouse. All eight of the contracted lighthouses were now complete.

Although rightfully proud of their accomplishments, Gibbons and Kelly were in for a shock, as were government inspectors and lighthouse officials. When the Fresnel lenses intended for the new light stations arrived by ship from Europe, it quickly became apparent that they could not be squeezed into the lanterns atop the towers of any of the lighthouses. The lanterns and in some cases, the towers themselves, were too small to accommodate the enormous prismatic lenses. Most of the lighthouses had to be renovated, and the towers at Point Conception and on the Farallon Islands had to be torn down and completely rebuilt. Gibbons and Kelly had contracted to build the lighthouses for $15,000 each. The cost of renovations and rebuilding, added to the cost incurred from the loss of the *Oriole*, doubtless more than wiped out any profit the Baltimore businessmen had hoped to make.

Despite all these difficulties, however, the new maritime lights were soon shining. The first western beacon in service was the one at Alcatraz, where, on June 1, 1854, the keeper lit the lamp inside the sparkling new lens. A sheet of bright light reached out across the formerly dark waters of San Francisco Bay, ushering in a new and safer era of navigation in the West.

Part One

ROMANTIC BEACONS OF THE OLYMPIC HEADLANDS

Washington

It has been said that *no man is an island,* but this poetic notion attributed to the seventeenth-century British clergyman John Donne, apparently does not apply to lighthouse keepers. For these brave men and women, especially those who served at remote light stations in the West, life was indeed an island. Surviving on low government salaries, they lived mostly on wild headlands and treeless ledges very far from what most of us would call civilization. Often the closest town was itself a backwater, a remote outpost. In bad weather, even the nearest rural church might seem impossibly distant.

When storms rushed in from the ocean, as they often did, lighthouse keepers could not follow the example of the mariners they served and run for some calm harbor. Because their ships had stone foundations and no engines, sails, rudders, or helms, they had to stay and take whatever the sea threw at them. To fight back against gale and gloom, they had only their lights and their wits. The lamps, which often stood at the top of winding staircases with hundreds of steps, were in constant need of attention. But whatever the conditions or the health of the keeper, they had to be kept burning. As a result, keepers always worked nights and rarely had a day off.

Lighthouse keepers endured this sort of existence, not necessarily for any high-minded or romantic reason—for instance, because they

Among the oldest of the West's navigational beacons, Cape Disappointment Light marks the entrance to the mighty Columbia River.
ZHUQIN CHEN/E+ VIA GETTY IMAGES

loved the sea, the wind, or the isolation—but for the same reason most people work: It rewarded them with a place to live and a smattering of pay. It was also a job worth doing, a job that had to be done.

Few, if any, of America's hundreds of light stations were ever lonelier or more vital to safe navigation than the one on Washington's Cape Flattery. Beaming seaward from a barren island many miles from the nearest house or settlement, the Cape Flattery beacon marks not only the entrance to the Strait of Juan de Fuca but also the far northwestern corner of the contiguous United States. This strategically placed lighthouse was built in 1857, several years before the Civil War, and the station remains in operation today, having served mariners for the better part of two centuries. During much of that time, resident keepers tended the beacon and kept the light burning through storms and months long sieges of dense fog.

As at other remote light stations, both individual keepers and families were assigned to Cape Flattery, and some found the isolation all but unendurable. During the late 1890s, one Cape Flattery keeper found life on these faraway rocks so lonely that he decided to put a sudden end to his misery. In a moment of complete desperation, he jumped off one of the cape's precipitous cliffs. Although he fell more than 100 feet onto the wave swept boulders below, some miracle spared his life. His assistant keeper later found him lying unconscious on the rocks and carried him to safety, and he later recovered from his injuries both physical and psychological.

The State of Washington has more than 3,000 miles of coastline and, consequently, more than a few lighthouses. Some are in or near urban areas such as Seattle, but most are on islands or remote promontories. Nearly all were, like the Cape Flattery Lighthouse, once served by rather lonely full-time keepers. All have long since been automated by the U.S. Coast Guard, so keepers are no longer in residence. Even so, these faithful beacons continue to guide mariners and to inspire lighthouse aficionados who either find a way to visit them or, at least, can see their lights shining in the distance.

Lights of the San Juan Islands: Northwest Washington State

Among America's foremost scenic treasures are the San Juans, a chain of lovely and mostly unspoiled islands situated to the northeast of the Strait of Juan de Fuca between the United States and Canada. Pleasure boaters, yachtsmen, and ferry pilots who navigate the tangle of narrow passages that separate the 172 separate islands and islets know the channels here can be narrow and dangerous, especially at night. Nearly all such small boat captains now rely on the precision of navigational software. However,

Turn Point Light
1893

they are nonetheless happy for the assistance of the handful of maritime beacons that still brighten these waters.

Among the lighthouses and beacons that remain in operation in or near the San Juans is the Turn Point Light, established in 1893. Its light shines from atop a squat, sixteen-foot concrete tower on the northwest end of Stuart Island. The thirty-eight-foot wooden tower of the Patos Island Lighthouse, completed in 1908, stands on the

Patos Island Light
1908

western side of a scenic, 260-acre islet in the northern part of the chain. The octagonal tower of Lime Kiln Lighthouse dates from 1914 and marks the key shipping channel through Haro Strait. Built in 1906, the thirty-four-foot wood-frame Burrows Island Lighthouse, has marked the southern entrance to Rosario Strait for more than a century. Cattle Point Lighthouse marks the southern end of San Juan Island.

Lime Kiln Light
1914

Burrows Island Light
1906

Cattle Point Light
1935

LIDIJA KAMANSKY/MOMENT OPEN VIA GETTY IMAGES

How to Get There

Information on ferry or float plane access to Friday Harbor on San Juan Island and other nearby ports of call is available at visitsanjuans.com. The Washington State Ferry Service provides regular access to the largest islands; call (206) 464–6400. The comfortable ferries often provide excellent views of one or more lighthouses.

Admiralty Head Light
Whidbey Island, Washington
1861 and 1903

Completed during the months just prior to the Civil War, the original Admiralty Head Lighthouse ranked among the West's earliest navigational markers. The frame structure was built atop a knob called Red Bluff. Its tower rose 41 feet from base to lantern, and it had a fourth-order Fresnel lens. The station's fixed white light, which could be seen from about 16 miles away, welcomed Puget Sound marine traffic into Admiralty Inlet.

During the Spanish-American War, the U.S. Army demolished the old lighthouse to make room for fortifications on Red Bluff intended to protect the entrance to the inlet. The present Spanish-style structure was ready for service by 1903 but would remain active for only about 25 years. Nowadays, the carefully restored lighthouse serves as a museum.

How to Get There
The lighthouse is part of Fort Casey State Park, not far from the Keystone/Port Townsend ferry slip and a few miles from the historic island town of Coupeville. For more information visit parks.wa.gov. Ferries approaching Admiralty Island provide excellent views of views of the Admiralty Head Lighthouse; call (206) 464–6400.

Point Wilson Light
Port Townsend, Washington
1879 and 1914

Typically, nineteenth-century sailing ships approached Port Townsend along the calmer eastern shore of Admiralty Inlet and were guided into port by the Admiralty Head Light. However, steam-powered ships favored the inlet's western shore where the water was deeper. To guide these deeper-draft vessels, the government established the Point Wilson Light. It had a fourth-order Fresnel lens and produced a beacon visible from any point along a sweeping 270 degrees of horizon.

Eventually, erosion threatened to undercut the tower, and in 1914 a new 46-foot, octagonal masonry tower replaced the original wooden lighthouse. Set a safe distance from water's edge, the 1914 lighthouse still stands. The station's classic fourth-order lens with its ruby-glass red sector remains in use.

How to Get There

The lighthouse is adjacent to Fort Worden State Park at the far northeastern end of the Olympic Peninsula. Take Route 20 to Port Townsend and then follow signs to the park. For more information visit fortworden.org or call (360) 344–4400.

Point No Point Light
Hansville, Washington
1879

Mariners moving from Puget Sound into Admiralty Inlet may notice a prominent headland sweeping up from the southwest. Often mistaken for other nearby features, it has long been known as Point No Point. Since 1879, a key navigational light has shone from this oddly named landfall.

Built on a 40-acre tract originally acquired for a mere $1,800, the Point No Point Lighthouse is a near twin of its sister station on West Point, near Seattle. It features a short rectangular tower attached to a fog signal building and a separate keeper's dwelling. The fourth-order bull's-eye Fresnel lens that once focused the flashing Point No Point beacon remains in place. However, the beacon is now produced by an automated modern optic placed on a pole a short distance from the tower.

Over the years, the Point No Point Lighthouse saved many ships from disaster. One that it could not save was the small passenger liner *Admiral Sampson*, which sank off the point in 1914 after colliding with a second liner, the *Princess Victoria*. Eleven passengers and crew went down with the *Admiral Sampson*, including Captain Zimro Moore.

How to Get There

From Port Gamble follow Highway 104 south and then Highway 305 east. Then turn north onto Hansville Road and follow it for approximately 10 miles to the town of Hansville. Signs point the way to the lighthouse, which is now available for overnight stays. For more information visit the United States Lighthouse Society website at uslhs .org or call (415) 362–7255.

Mukilteo Light
Mukilteo, Washington
1906

Mukilteo is a Native American word meaning "good spot for camping." Early in the twentieth century, the US Lighthouse Service decided that Mukilteo was also a good location for a lighthouse to guide vessels to the port of Everett. Completed in 1906, the Victorian-style structure was fitted with a fourth-order Fresnels lens and equipped with a steam-powered trumpet to warn ships plowing blindly through the dense fog that often blankets Puget Sound. The historic lens remains in place and still focuses the station's beacon, which flashes every five seconds. The City of Mukilteo now owns and maintains the lighthouse property and structures.

How to Get There

The lighthouse, located at 608 Front Street in Mukilteo, contains a photographic exhibit on the lights of the Puget Sound. Located near the Whidbey Island ferry landing, the wood-frame structure is open to the public on weekends. For more information visit mukilteo historical.org.

West Point Light
Seattle, Washington
1881

Located only five miles from the bustling heart of Seattle, the old West Point Lighthouse marks a low, sandy peninsula at the north entrance to Elliot Bay. For more than 140 years it has pointed the way in and out of the bay, thus helping to ensure the prosperity of Washington's thriving commercial hub. Today it also serves as a key attraction of the city's popular Discovery Park. Still focused by its historic fourth-order Fresnel lens, the station's flashing light remains in service.

How to Get There
The lighthouse is located about a mile and half from the entrance of Seattle's Discovery Park. Excellent views of the lighthouse can be had via a pleasant stroll along West Point Beach. For more information visit seattle.gov/parks or call (206) 386–4236.

Alki Point Light
Seattle, Washington
1887 and 1913

Alki Point, south of Seattle, was once marked by a simple kerosene lantern hung from the side of a barn.

A wedge-shaped peninsula known as Alki Point threatens shipping moving through Puget Sound toward Seattle and is especially dangerous during stretches of heavy fog that frequently blanket these waters. To assist mariners, an early local farmer regularly hung a kerosene lantern on the door of his barn. No one can say how many wrecks this "cow beacon" may have prevented.

In 1887, with shipping traffic between Seattle and Tacoma to the south on the increase, the government established an official, though still modest, navigational light here. The beacon, produced by a small lantern poised atop a wooden post, served for more than twenty-five years. Finally, in 1913, Alki Point received a true lighthouse. Consisting of an octagonal, thirty-seven-foot-tall masonry tower, attached fog-signal building, and nearby keeper's dwelling, it still stands and remains in use today.

For many years the station employed a fourth-order Fresnel lens, but it was replaced by a modern aerobeacon in 1962. It is said the original lens was stolen by an antique dealer but reclaimed some years later by the U.S. Coast Guard, which placed it in a Seattle museum. A replica is now on display at the lighthouse.

How to Get There

Alki Lighthouse is located just south of the public beach at Alki which can be reached from Seattle via I–5 south, and the West Seattle Freeway. Although the lighthouse is an active Coast Guard facility, it is open to the public on Saturday and Sunday afternoons during the summer. For more information visit www.uscga-seattle.com.

Point Robinson Light
Tacoma, Washington
1887 and 1915

The captains of vessels plying the heavily trafficked waters of Puget Sound between Seattle and Tacoma watch closely for the Point Robinson Light. Located on the eastern end of Maury Island, the light marks a key safe channel in this narrow but crowded channel.

A fog signal was placed on the point in 1885 to prevent ships from running aground on Maury Island. Particularly threatening was a low, sandy spit extending several hundred yards out into Puget Sound. Maritime officials soon concluded that the fog signal alone was inadequate, and in 1887 a modest lantern and lens were added to the station.

As shipping increased in the lower Puget Sound, the station's importance grew. In 1915 a fully equipped lighthouse was established here. It consisted of a pair of keeper's dwellings and a 38-foot masonry and concrete tower, a near twin of the tower on Alki Point a few miles to the north.

With its peaceful, scenic location and proximity to Tacoma and Seattle, Robinson Point Lighthouse was once a very popular duty station for keepers and their families. Nowadays, the light is automated and does its job without the help of resident keepers.

How to Get There
The lighthouse is located on the banks of the Puget Sound at the northeast corner of Maury Island just across from the larger and more populous Vachon Island. Leased by King County from the U.S. Coast Guard, which maintains the original Fresnel lens, the station is open to the public as part of the Vashon Park District. For more information visit www.vashonparkdistrict.org.

New Dungeness Light
Sequim, Washington
1857

A five-mile-long blade of sand known as the Dungeness Spit juts northward from the Olympic Peninsula threatening vessels moving through the Strait of Juan de Fuca. Rising only a few feet above high tide, the spit is all but invisible to ships. To help prevent them from running aground, maritime authorities established a lighthouse here in 1857.

Rising though the center of its attached, two-story keeper's dwelling, the New Dungeness tower is 63 feet tall.

During its early years, the light guided not only ships and fishing boats but also canoes paddled by Native American warriors prepared to do battle with one another on the spit. Traditionally, tribes living on opposite sides of the Strait of Juan de Fuca would meet on the spit to settle their differences. After the lighthouse was built, they continued this practice, but now their meeting place was much easier to find. Apparently happy to have a light to guide them, the war parties never molested the keepers—only one another.

The lighthouse and the spit took their names from Dungeness Point in England, coincidentally famed for its own magnificent lighthouse. Like its British namesake, Dungeness Spit is a ship killer, and over the years, many vessels were lost in its sands. The New Dunfeness beacon slowed, but did not altogether stop these losses. The New Dungeness Light, originally focused by a classic Fresnel lens, is now generated by a modern optic.

How to Get There

The lighthouse is accessible only by boat or by means of a five-mile hike along the scenic Dungeness Spit, now part of the Dungeness Wildlife Refuge. This highly worthwhile adventure begins at the refuge parking area and takes about five hours round-trip. The hike should only be attempted in good weather at low tide. For more information visit newdungenesslighthouse.com or call (360) 683–6638.

Cape Flattery Light
Cape Flattery, Washington
1857

The Cape Flattery Light marks the far northwestern corner of the contiguous (lower 48) United States as well as the entrance to the commercially vital Strait of Juan De Fuca. The beacon shines out into the dark Pacific from barren Tatoosh Island where generations of lonely lighthouse keepers served for months, years, or even decades at a time. The 65-foot sandstone tower and Cape Cod–style dwelling stand as a testament to the hardiness of those keepers and their families who often lived here with them.

Among the West's first great navigational sentinels, this lighthouse was completed and placed in operation in 1857. The stone tower rose directly out of the keeper's dwelling so that station personnel could climb its steps and keep the light burning without braving the harsh Tatoosh Island weather. The original first-order Fresnel lens had been intended for Old Point Loma in Southern California. However, its brass frame proved much too large for the modest Point Loma tower, so the lens was shipped to Cape Flattery instead.

Maintaining the enormous polished-crystal lens took considerable effort requiring keepers to serve here full-time until the station was automated 1977. Today, the Cape Flattery Lighthouse no longer displays the station's beacon as it is produced by a modern rotating optic positioned on a 30-foot-high skeletal tower. Now part of the Makah Native American Reservation, Tatoosh Island is part of a marine sanctuary.

How to Get There
Inaccessible from the land, the station can be seen from the water or from a trail on the Makah Reservation at the end of Route 112. The trail requires several steep climbs and moderate physical exertion.

Destruction Island Light
Destruction Island, Washington
1891

During the eighteenth century, a Native American war party killed several seamen who had gone ashore here to fill casks with fresh water. Afterward, this wilderness landfall would always be known as Destruction Island, and the ominous moniker proved an apt one. Over the years the boulder-strewn island, often hidden under heavy blankets of fog, has exacted a heavy toll in ships and lives.

As early as 1855 the Lighthouse Board saw need for a powerful navigational light to warn ships away from Destruction Island. However, building a lighthouse on this remote and rugged offshore site proved such a daunting task that the project was delayed for more than 30 years. A steady increase in shipping along the Washington coast and the lengthening list of wrecks on the jagged rocks of Destruction Island finally forced the government to act and construction got underway in 1888.

Building this extraordinarily remote lighthouse was hard work. Materials had to be brought ashore in small boats from a tender anchored in a cove near the construction site. Workers suffered continually from rain and cold, and lack of supplies was a chronic problem. Even so, the tower, dwelling, and outbuildings were completed within three years, and the station's fog signal and beacon became operational late in 1891.

Because of its isolation, Destruction Island was never a popular duty station for keepers. No doubt, the last full-time Destruction Island keepers were greatly relieved when the station was automated in 1968 and they were assigned to lighthouses in more populated areas. The classic Destruction Island first-order lens was removed in 1995, and the station was shut down altogether in 2008.

How to Get There

Although the Destruction Island Lighthouse is off-limits to the public, it can be seen from a parking area along US 101, about a mile south of Ruby Beach. Destruction Island and its lighthouse are now under the management of the US Fish and Wildlife Service as part of the Quillayute Needles National Wildlife Refuge.

Grays Harbor Light
Westport, Washington
1898

Rising more than 100 feet from base to lantern, the octagonal, brick Grays Harbor Lighthouse ranks among the tallest on the Pacific coast. The light, still focused by the station's original third-order Fresnel lens, serves as a major coastal light and guides vessels to the harbor and fishing town of Westport. The lens has three bull's-eyes about eight inches in diameter emitting alternating white and red flashes. The height of the tower and power of the lens make the beacon visible from up to 21 miles away.

How to Get There
Popular with photographers, the lighthouse is closed to the public except on holiday weekends during summer, but it can be viewed anytime from Ocean Avenue in the delightful seaside town of Westport or from the Westport Maritime Museum, a former U.S. Coast Guard lifeboat station. For more information, visit westportmaritimemuseum.com or call (360) 268–0078.

The Gray's Harbor beacon emits alternating white and red flashes.

North Head Light
Ilwaco, Washington
1898

The mouth of the Columbia River threatens mariners with an extensive bar which has claimed many vessels large and small. Established in 1898, the North Head Light was intended to warn ships approaching the Columbia and its destructive bar from the north. The lighthouse features a white 65-foot tower poised near the edge of a 130-foot-high cliff. The combined height of the tower and cliff places the beacon almost 200 feet above the Pacific.

Originally fitted with a first-order classic lens removed from the nearby Cape Disappointment Lighthouse, it received a less powerful fourth-order lens in 1930. Nowadays, a rotating aeromarine beacon produces the beacon.

North Head is said to be the windiest spot in America. Gusts of up to 150 miles per hour are said to blast across the narrow peninsula. Trees, chimneys, and fences have been flattened by these gale-force winds. In 1932 a wild duck, blown off course by the wind, smashed into the lantern, shattering windows, and chipping the glass prisms of the lens. The damaged equipment was soon repaired, but the unfortunate duck was a complete loss.

How to Get There

From the town of Ilwaco off US 101, follow the signs to Cape Disappointment State Park. Markers point the way to the lighthouse. The park's Lewis and Clark Interpretive Center houses what is thought to be the first-order Fresnel lens that served at Cape Disappointment from 1856 to 1898 and at North Head from 1898 until 1932. The lighthouse grounds are open free of charge year-round, dawn until dusk. For more information visit northheadlighthouse.com.

Cape Disappointment Light
Ilwaco, Washington
1856

This cape received its strangely melancholy name from fur trader John Meares, who mistook the headland for another landfall farther south—the one now named for him—and sailed away in disappointment. The captains of many other ships have encountered another a more bitter form of disappointment at this cape. Countless vessels have foundered here and on the nearby Columbia River Bar.

As early as 1848, Federal surveyors designated Cape Disappointment as the site of one of the West's first major light stations. However, building a lighthouse on the isolated and wind-blasted cape proved far more difficult and expensive than they imagined. During the fall of 1853, the bark *Oriole* foundered on the Columbia River Bar while attempting to deliver materials for the tower. A year would pass before a second shipment arrived and further delays were caused by incessant downpours and voracious mud that consumed whole wagonloads of supplies. Finally, in October 1856, the 53-foot, dressed-stone conical tower was completed, and the oil lamps inside its first-order Fresnel lens were lit.

In 1898 the Cape Disappointment Lighthouse lost its classic first-order lens to the recently completed light station on nearby North Head. A fourth-order Fresnel optic served here until 1937 when it was replaced by the present marine rotating beacon.

Cape Disappointment. FRANCESCO VANINETTI PHOTO/MOMENT VIA GETTY IMAGES

How to Get There

From Ilwaco follow signs for Cape Disappointment State Park. Visitors can reach the lighthouse via a short hike from the parking area. The park's Lewis and Clark Interpretive Center celebrates the famous explorers and their visit to the cape nearly two centuries ago. The original Cape Disappointment first-order Fresnel lens is on display at the center. For more information visit capedisappointment.org or call (360) 642–3078.

Part Two

ROMANTIC BEACONS OF THE EMERALD COAST

Oregon

During the early 1880s, tough government construction crews completed one of the boldest building projects ever undertaken, the castle-like lighthouse that sits atop rugged Tillamook Rock just off the coast of Oregon. They succeeded despite human opposition onshore and, perhaps, inhuman opponents on the rock itself. However, the lighthouse they built was never a very comfortable place for the keepers who lived hard, solitary lives out on the barren one-acre rock. The lighthouse was cramped, cold, and exposed to the most terrible weather imaginable. Even worse, in the minds and hearts of some keepers, it was thought to be haunted. Many locals still believe the rock and its long-abandoned light station are indeed haunted. And who would argue the point? For decades, the otherwise empty lighthouse has been used as a columbarium, a place where the cremated ashes of the dead are stored.

As an outpost of human endeavor, the Tillamock Rock Lighthouse was always as much a symbol as a navigational aid. It marked not only a dangerous maritime hazard but also the precarious and shifting border between human enterprise and the forces of nature and, as some might say, the unnatural.

Located more than a mile offshore, near Oregon's magnificent Tillamock Head and about 20 miles south of the Columbia River, this storm-dashed bastion clings to a scrap of rock caught almost totally in the grip of an all-too-often unfriendly ocean. In a gale, mountainous waves sweep over the rock and pound the walls of the lighthouse. Few buildings anywhere in the world are so exposed to the whims and power of wind, weather, and sea. Yet the Tillamook Lighthouse has stood, more or less intact, since 1881.

Completed during the horse and buggy days before the era of automobiles, airplanes, helicopters, computers, electrical power tools, or diesel-powered drilling and earthmoving equipment, this amazing structure surely ranks among the foremost engineering triumphs of all time. There were many during the nineteenth century who said the lighthouse could never be built and more than a few others who said it *should* never be built. Among the latter were Native Americans who claimed evil spirits resided there.

Naturally enough, the government maritime officials who ordered construction of the lighthouse completely dismissed the notion that any spirits resided on Tillamock Rock, evil or otherwise. However, the hardy construction crews who shouldered the task of building the lighthouse may not have agreed. Not long after the work began in early September 1879, a popular master mason from nearby Portland was killed while surveying the rugged construction site. Learning of this, construction laborers could only be enticed to go ashore on Tillamook by the offer of substantial bonus pay.

Many who took the money would later curse themselves for their greed. Storms and high winds drove away the project tender *Corwin*, leaving them stranded for days or even weeks at a time without food or fuel. Miserable experiences of this sort drove some workers away, but the toughest refused to quit even after hurricane-force winds sent giant waves pounding over the rock threatening to wash the crew into the sea. They gritted their teeth, held on, and when the winds died down again, returned to the business of building the lighthouse.

During the summer, the basalt walls began to take shape. The tower, residence, and workrooms were completed by late fall, just in time for the hardworking crew to take a brief Christmas break. Then, by January 1, 1881, they were back on the rock finishing the interior of the lighthouse and installing the station's enormous first-order Fresnel lens.

Before that New Years' Day had come to an end, however, a tremendous gale blew in from the northwest. That night the workers on the rock began to hear strange noises above the roar of the storm. They thought they heard the voices of men calling to them from the darkness, and they were sure they heard the sound of a dog barking. Suddenly, from out of the gloom, a large sailing ship came into view. It reeled first to port, then to starboard as the waves forced it onto the rocks. Then, as quickly as it had appeared, the ship was gone.

On the next day with the storm passed and the sun shining brightly, the fate of the mystery ship and its crew became all too apparent. Its shattered remains littered the rocks of nearby Tillamook Head. The unlucky ship had been the *Lupatia*, bound from Japan to Oregon. The *Lupatia* had arrived, but not in the manner its captain and crew had intended. None aboard the *Lupatia* survived except for the ship's dog, who later took up residence at the lighthouse.

This disaster served as a sobering reminder of just how important it was to establish a navigational beacon here. A beacon on Tillamook Rock might spell the difference between life and death for mariners they did not know and would never meet. No doubt such thoughts chilled and depressed the construction crew. Had they finished their work just a few days earlier, the beacon might have been in operation soon enough to save the *Lupatia*. Ironically, its lamps were first lit just ten days later. Although saddened, the construction crew moved ahead with their work putting the finishing touches on the project. The station's beacon remained in service for the next 76 years. Although not all as storied or magnificent as the Tillamook Head Light, most of Oregon's lighthouse still guide mariners.

Lightship *Columbia*
Astoria, Oregon
1951

Lightships were intended to warn mariners away from dangerous offshore obstacles that could not be easily marked from land.

Among the last of America's lightships, the 128-foot *Columbia* was launched in Maine in 1951. For nearly three decades she rode the waves on station eight miles off the dangerous Columbia River bar. Retired in 1979, she has since served as the prime attraction of the Columbia River Maritime Museum in Astoria.

How to Get There
The lightship is moored near the Columbia River Maritime Museum at 1792 Marine Drive, Astoria, OR 97103. For more information visit crmm.org or call (503) 325–2323.

Cape Meares Light
Tillamook, Oregon
1890

The lighthouse that now stands on Cape Meares was built in the wrong place. Originally intended for Cape Lookout, the station ended up on Cape Meares because of a mapmaker's error. The two names had been reversed on U.S. Coast Survey charts, and dismayed officials did not discover the mistake until the station was almost complete. Rather than incur the cost of building an entirely new facility on Cape Lookout, the Lighthouse Service decided to leave well enough alone.

Only 38 feet tall, the octagonal iron-sheathed brick tower stood at the edge of a cliff, placing the focal plane of its light 215 feet above the breakers. A huge first-order Fresnel lens, for many years illuminated by a coal-oil lamp, made the light visible from 21 miles at sea. Deactivated in 1963, the old lighthouse is now a popular tourist attraction. Much to their discredit, vandals have damaged the magnificent lens on more than one occasion.

How to Get There

Located in Cape Meares State Park, the lighthouse can be reached via Three Capes Loop Road, off US 101 at Tillamook. For more information visit friendsofcapemeareslighthouse.org or call (503) 842–2244.

Yaquina Bay Light
Newport, Oregon
1871

Built on the crest of a hill near the entrance to Yaquina Bay, the lamps in the little red lantern atop this wood-frame lighthouse first burned in November 1871. Less than three years later they were permanently snuffed out when construction of a larger lighthouse at Yaquina Head made the light redundant. Perhaps surprisingly, the old lighthouse was never torn down and has survived for more than 150 years. The structure has been handsomely restored but is not currently open to the public.

How to Get There

The Yaquina Bay Lighthouse is located near the north end of the Yaquina Bay Bridge in Yaquina Bay State Park. Together with the Friends of Yaquina Lighthouses, the U.S. Forest Service maintains the structure. For further information visit yaquinalights.org or call (541) 574–3100.

Yaquina Head Light
Newport, Oregon
1873

Shortly after the Yaquina Bay Lighthouse first guided vessels in and out of the harbor at Newport in 1871, maritime officials concluded that a more powerful coastal light was needed to protect vessels moving along this dangerous stretch of the Oregon coast. The best location for such a beacon turned out to be Yaquina Head a few miles north of Newport. The 93-foot tower was built atop an emerald-green headland dropping straight down into the roiling Pacific. So beautiful is this historic lighthouse and its setting that it daily causes hundreds of dazzled motorists on nearby Highway 1 to pull over and take a photograph. Completed in 1873, the new lighthouse was given a huge, 12-foot-high classic Fresnel lens which has graced the lantern room for more than 150 years. It still shines today, casting seaward a beam visible from 19 miles away.

How to Get There
Located about 4 miles north of Newport off US 101, the station is often open to the public. For more information visit yaquinalights.org or call (541) 574–3100. The area around the lighthouse is part of an attractive Bureau of Land Management natural area.

Heceta Head Light
Near Florence, Oregon
1894

It took decades to establish an unbroken string of maritime lights along the entire 1,500-mile length of the West Coast. One of the last dark stretches was a 90-mile stretch of bleak and foggy shoreline to the south of Newport, Oregon. The navigators of ships plying these waters were left to find their way in the dark. More than a few such vessels likely ended their days here vanishing without a trace along with their hapless crews. But in the spring of 1894 help arrived in the form of bright maritime light shining from atop a 56-foot white masonry tower perched on the Heceta Head cliffs just north of the Oregon port of Florence.

Building a lighthouse in this rugged and remote location took nearly two years and $180,000—a fantastic sum at the time. Construction materials had to be brought in by ship to the nearby Suislaw River and then hauled by mule-drawn wagon to the construction site.

Once complete, the new lighthouse was fitted with an exquisite first-order Fresnel lens with 640 individual prisms. Originally, the light came from a five-wick, coal-oil lamp. A weighted cable powered the gears that turned the lamp, causing the light to

Heceta Head Lighthouse. FRANCESCO VANINETTI PHOTO/MOMENT VIA GETTY IMAGES

flash. Although the old lamp has given way to a million-candlepower electric bulb, the original classic lens still shines. Its beam flashes seaward from an elevation of more than 200 feet and can be seen from up to 21 miles.

How to Get There

One of the most scenic light stations in the West, Heceta Head Lighthouse is popular with photographers. It stands on a craggy point about 11 miles north of Florence. Turn off US 101 at Devils Elbow State Park. For those who think lighthouses are romantic, Heceta Head has a treat in store as the old keeper's residence is now a delightful bed-and-breakfast inn. For more information visit hecetalighthouse.com or call (866) 547–3696.

Umpqua River Light
Winchester Bay, Oregon
1857 and 1894

The conical, plaster-covered masonry tower rises just above the treetops of a state park named in its honor. At night the flashing light, alternating red and white, can be seen from 21 miles away. The existing tower dates to 1894, but a lighthouse stood here as early as 1857.

Erected under the constant threat of attack by Native Americans, the first Umpqua River tower lasted only four years. Floods quickly undercut its foundation, and in 1861 it collapsed into the river. Nothing was done to revive the station until the 1890s. Completed in 1894 from the same plans as the Heceta Head Lighthouse, the present 67-foot tower was crowned with the same powerful, first-order Fresnel lens that still serves here today. The site, located safely above the river, raises the focal plane of the light 165 feet above the sea.

How to Get There
Managed by Douglas County, the light can be seen and enjoyed from the adjacent Umpqua River Lighthouse State Park, located off US 101 just south of Winchester Bay. A fine visitors' center with museum occupies the former Umpqua River Coast Guard Station. For information visit umpquavalleymuseums.org or call (541) 271–4631.

Cape Arago Light
Charleston, Oregon
1866, 1909, and 1934

A lighthouse stood on Oregon's Cape Arago as early as the 1860s, but the current structure dates to the 1930. Decommissioned in 2008, the old lighthouse is inaccessible and off limits to visitors. However, it can be seen at a distance from Sunset Bay State Park near the town of Charleston.

Coquille River Light
Bandon, Oregon
1896

Located in Bullards Beach State Park near Bandon, the Coquille River Lighthouse was established in 1896 and then abandoned in 1939. Although gutted by a mysterious fire, it has been restored, and a decorative light now shines from its tower at night.

Cape Blanco Light
Port Orford, Oregon
1870

Cape Blanco and its light station likely take their names from the precipitous white cliffs that drop almost vertically down to the beaches nearly 200 feet below the lighthouse. Oldest and southernmost of Oregon's major beacons, the light shines from atop a 59-foot conical tower erected in 1870. The considerable height of the cliffs raises the focal plane of the light to a lofty 245 feet above mean sea level. Focused by a second-order Fresnel lens, the light can be seen from up to 22 miles at sea. Vandals ravaged the classic lens in 1992, doing more than $500,000 in damage, but fortunately, the lens has been replaced.

How to Get There
The lighthouse is located near Cape Blanco State Park, off US 101 a few miles north of Port Orford. Visitors are welcome to walk the grounds when the light station is open. For more information visit oregonstateparks.gov or enjoyportorford.com.

Part Three

ROMANTIC BEACONS OF THE REDWOOD CLIFFS

Northern California

Along the 840 miles of the California coastline, the transition from land to water is sudden and dangerous. In many places lofty desert mountains drop straight down into the waves, and offshore, lesser peaks rise from the ocean floor to lurk just beneath the surface. The prevailing westerly winds are likely to drive vessels much closer to shore than their captains intend, all too often with deadly results. The California coast is such a threat to mariners that, unless they are headed for port, most plot a course many miles from the nearest landfall.

To help navigators maintain a respectful distance and find safe harbor, the US government established a string of powerful navigational beacons along the rugged shores from San Diego all the way to Crescent City. The first of these California lighthouses were built in 1850s only a few years after the gold rush. Before that time, however, the California coast was dark and largely uncharted. Indeed, for centuries California was so poorly understood that many mapmakers and mariners, believed it was an island.

Although he had never seen it, sixteenth-century Spanish novelist Montalvo described California as an island inhabited entirely by warrior women *robust of body, strong and passionate in heart, and of great valor. Their island is one of the most rugged in the world with bold rocks and crags. Their arms are all of gold as are the harnesses of the wild beasts, which after taming, they ride. In all the island there is no other metal.* Enthralled by these romantic notions, early Spanish explorers put them to the test by trying to sail completely around the "Island of California." They never succeeded, of course, and much to their disappointment, likewise failed to locate a single member of Montalvo's tribe of gold-laden Amazons. However, Montalvo's description of the California coast as among *the most rugged in the world with bold rocks and crags* proved all too accurate. Over the centuries, it would crush the wooden hulls of hundreds of Spanish sailing ships and claim the lives of countless sailors.

Likely, the adventurer Juan Rodriguez Cabrillo knew better than to accept Montalvo's more fanciful claims at face value when he sailed from Navidad in western Mexico (New Spain) in June 1542, just half a century after Columbus arrived in America. With two small ships, the *Victoria and Salvador,* and a combined crew of about 250, Cabrillo pushed slowly northward, reaching San Diego Bay in late September. Cabrillo and his men then made their way up the coast as far north as present-day Oregon before finally turning for home—a destination the explorer would never reach. Cabrillo died from injuries received in a fall he took on shore, probably somewhere near Point Reyes. However, Cabrillo's expedition succeeded in bringing the first Europeans to California and proving beyond reasonable doubt that it was not an island and not inhabited by a mysterious race of Amazons. He and his men accomplished all of this without the aid of charts or even the faintest flicker of a navigational light.

The First California Beacons

A trickle of Spanish ranchers, Franciscan missionaries (Father Junipero Serra's sandaled Padres), and soldiers followed Cabrillo to California. They built no lighthouses, but instead lit fires on Point Loma and elsewhere along the coast to call their ships in from the sea. To mark channels and guide supply vessels to the mission and presidio at San Diego, bright candles were hung from poles; otherwise, the king's mariners were forced to navigate the dangerous coast without the help of lights calling to them from the shore. But the California coast would grow brighter in time, especially after gold was discovered in the California foothills and Mexico ceded the province to the United States in 1848.

The beckoning glitter of California's gold fields profoundly changed the way Americans viewed the West. No longer seen primarily as a mostly empty place where formerly landless Easterners could carve out hardscrabble homesteads, it was now thought of as an opportunity to get rich quick. The California gold rush was on, and countless thousands of panhandlers, merchants, and other Forty-Niners headed West. Many if not most would reach California by ship—if they reached it at all.

During the gold rush era, scores of San Francisco–bound passenger ships and freighters got lost in the fog or gloom and were dashed to bits on California's deadly rocks. Among the more notable of these wrecks were those of the *Caroline Amelia* in 1850, the *Winfield Scott* in 1853, the *Yankee Blade* and *Golden Fleece* in 1854, and the *Granada* in 1860. In these and many similar disasters, hundreds, perhaps even thousands of lives were lost to the waves along with countless millions of dollars in ships and property. As these losses mounted, US government officials became increasing alarmed. The nation could never hope to settle and exploit the West without a secure coastline, inviting to maritime commerce. Making the California coast safe for navigation required construction of numerous lighthouses, many of which had to be built under extremely dangerous and trying circumstances.

St. George Battles the Dragon

Perhaps the most difficult task that would ever face Western lighthouse builders was construction of the light station on St. George Reef, a few miles west of Crescent City, California, near the far northern corner of the state. In 1792, English explorer George Vancouver charted these waters and made special note of an exceptionally dangerous offshore obstacle he named Dragon Rocks. Some local fishermen and other wary mariners still refer to it as "the Dragon" and for good reason. Usually, when vessels large or small fall into the jaws of this monster, only a few bits of wreckage will be left over to wash up on nearby beaches. The rest is swallowed forever by the ocean.

The name of this maritime menace was eventually changed to St. George Reef, a reference to the mythical medieval saint best known for slaying dragons. Ironically, St. George Reef is far more devil than saint and not really a reef at all, but rather a submerged volcanic mountain the uppermost rocks of which rise abruptly from the sea just above the toss of the waves. During heavy weather, breaking waves throw an obscuring blanket of mist over these rocks, rendering them all but invisible and offering mariners no hint of impending disaster.

Such were the conditions on July 30, 1865, just a few weeks after the end of the Civil War, when a big, clumsy sidewheeler known as *Brother Jonathan* plowed directly into St. George Reef. The *Jonathan* had been bound for San Francisco where many of its more than 200 passengers were due to disembark. Some were former Union and Confederate soldiers perhaps hoping to start a new life far from the blood-soaked battlefields of the East. Tragically, they would never get the chance as the *Jonathan's* hull was crushed and the vessel sank in a matter of minutes dragging nearly everyone aboard down into the depths of the Pacific. It is said the screams of drowning passengers and crew could be heard from miles away.

The outcry sparked by this tragedy convinced federal officials that something must be done to warn mariners. However, Lighthouse Board engineers had concluded that the only effective way to mark St. George Reef was to build a lighthouse directly over its exposed, wave-swept rocks. The challenge and cost of such an undertaking loomed so large that the project was delayed for more than fifteen years. Finally, during the early 1880s, the Board decided to move forward, placing construction in the hands of veteran government contractor M. A. Ballantyne, who had recently completed the offshore lighthouse on Oregon's Tillamook Rock.

During the winter of 1882, Ballantyne and his men arrived off St. George Reef in the 126-ton schooner *LaNinfa*. They had hoped the winter storms that typically sweep down on the Northern California coast would have passed by then, but they had not. For several weeks, the rough seas made it impossible to land men, materials, and equipment on the rocks, but by the early spring Ballantyne's tough 50-man crew had gained a toehold. Soon, his scrappy workers had rigged a cable from the schooner to the highest point of St. George Reef—about 54 feet—enabling them to use heavy mooring tackle to haul men and supplies just over the giant Pacific waves to the relative safety of the rocks.

The sea was not the only problem facing Ballantyne and his crew. The glycerin powder used for blasting out the foundation had to be handled with extreme care. One mistake might set off an explosion so destructive that it could obliterate the entire construction site. So, quite understandably, Ballantyne's workers took their time when using it. Another concern was the weather, which turned even more stormy than usual during the 1880s. Still another was money as the original appropriation ran out and additional funds were slow in coming. Not until 1887 did Congress provide sufficient funding to compete the project. The total bill for construction would mount to a whopping $704,633, more than $16 at today's dollar values, making this one of the most expensive lighthouses in the nation's history—and one of the hardest to build.

The St. George Reef Lighthouse was at last placed in service on October 20, 1892, more than ten years after construction got underway. The station was considered too isolated and dangerous for families, so most lighthouse personnel kept homes on the mainland. The station crew consisted of five men who worked four weeks on and two weeks off. For obvious reasons, St. George Lighthouse soon developed a reputation as one of the least popular and most dangerous light stations in America. On several occasions crewmen were killed while traveling to or from the lighthouse. In a single incident in 1951 three coastguardsmen were drowned when waves swamped the station launch.

In 1972 the Coast Guard abandoned the St. George Reef Lighthouse and replaced it with a buoy. The Dragon was then left unwatched to carry on its ceaseless battle with the sea. More recently, northern California lighthouse lovers have taken charge of the venerable lighthouse and are restoring it one wall, iron fitting, and window at a time. Their efforts are an appropriate monument to those who struggled or lost their lives to protect mariners from this ferocious navigational obstacle.

St. George Reef Light
Crescent City, California
1892

Built on an exposed rock constantly pounded by the Pacific, the exceedingly expensive St. George Reef Lighthouse took more than 10 years to complete. However, mariners who long dreaded this deadly obstacle no doubt thought the project well worth the time and expense. Over the centuries this notorious reef had ruined numerous ships including the side-wheeler *Brother Jonathan*, wrecked here in 1865 with a loss of more than 200 lives.

The hulking stone tower was erected on a giant elliptical base of granite and concrete. Rising more than 140 feet above the waves, the tower originally held a first-order Fresnel lens displaying an alternating red and white flashing light.

After the U.S. Coast Guard discontinued this light in 1975, local history buffs and lighthouse lovers wondered what would become of this legendary station. During the late 1990s they resolved to restore the historic station and to that purpose formed the St. George Reef Lighthouse Preservation Society. The effort suffered a setback in 2002 when the station's original lantern was accidentally destroyed while being moved ashore for restoration. Undeterred, the society had an exact replica built and placed atop the tower. Later that year the station's light was relit, and it now serves as a private aid to navigation.

How to Get There
This spectacular light station and its restored beacon can be seen from the end of Crescent City's Washington Boulevard. The station's 18-foot-high, first-order Fresnel lens is on display in the Del Norte County Historical Society Museum on Sixth Street in Crescent City; for additional information visit delnortehistory.org or call (707) 464–3922.

Battery Point Light
Crescent City, California
1856

Pressed by northern California lumber interests, Congress designated Crescent City as a site for one of the West's earliest lighthouses. Like many other Western light stations, this one consisted of a simple Cape Cod–style dwelling with a tower rising through the center of its roof. Beginning in 1856 the beacon, focused by its fourth-order Fresnel lens, guided freighters into the city's bustling harbor, then out again bearing loads of redwood lumber bound for San Francisco.

Captain John Jeffrey and his wife, Nellie, took over keeper's duties at the Crescent City Lighthouse in 1875. In all, they spent thirty-nine years in the lighthouse and raised four children there. The thick stone walls of the lighthouse, built for a mere $15,000, outlasted the Jeffrey family and several succeeding generations of keepers. They still stand today, little changed from the station's earliest days.

Except for a stroke of luck, however, the station's last night might have been that of March 27, 1964. The earthquake that hit Alaska on that date sent five titanic tidal waves hurtling toward the coast of northern California, where they stormed ashore shortly after midnight. Keepers Clarence and Peggy Coons saw them coming but were helpless in the face of what seemed certain disaster. Luck was with them as the enormous waves struck at such an extreme angle that the lighthouse and its keepers were spared.

Although discontinued in 1965, the light was reestablished in 1982 as a private aid to navigation. The building now serves as both a history museum and active lighthouse with resident keepers.

How to Get There

The lighthouse and museum are located at Battery Point on the west side of Crescent City Harbor. For additional information visit delnortehistory.org or call (707) 464-3922.

Trinidad Head Light
Trinidad, California
1871

Set on a jagged cliff face almost 200 feet above the Pacific, this little lighthouse has aided commercial anglers and other mariners seeking the shelter of Trinidad Harbor for more than 150 years. Built in 1871 to guide schooners carrying lumber to San Francisco, the light helped close a dark gap between Crescent City and Humboldt Bay to the south. While the station's fourth-order Fresnel lens was small for a coastal light, the elevation of the tower, which was perched on a high cliff, made its beacon visible from up to 20 miles at sea. When the light was automated in 1947, its classical lens was replaced by an airport-style beacon.

How to Get There
Take the Trinidad exit from US 101 and drive toward the harbor. The Trinidad Head Lighthouse is closed to the public, but hiking trails lead to an overlook with an excellent view of the old light station. Less energetic visitors have another attractive option: a replica of the tower has been built in town and is easy to find on foot. A near-perfect match of the original, it now houses the antique Fresnel lens that served for so many years at the official, but more difficult to reach Trinidad Head Lighthouse.

Table Bluff Light
Eureka, California
1892

After an earlier tower in Humboldt Harbor was severely damaged by a gale, it was replaced by a new lighthouse built atop nearby Table Bluff. A Victorian-style structure with an attached, square tower, it was given the same fourth-order lens that had once shone from the tower of the harbor lighthouse. Although the Table Bluff tower was only 35 feet tall, its elevation placed the light approximately 190 feet above the bay, enabling the light to be seen from up to 20 miles away.

Having served mariners for more than 80 years, the Table Bluff Lighthouse was decommissioned in 1972 and turned over to a private foundation. The little lighthouse was cut into two parts like an apple and trucked to Woodley Island near Eureka, where it was reassembled, repaired, and refitted with the station's old Fresnel lens. Today it serves as a tourist attraction and a reminder of the area's rich maritime history.

During nearly a century of service, the Table Bluff Lighthouse marked the entrance to Humboldt Bay, which provided access to Eureka, so named perhaps because the

SGOODWIN4813/ISTOCK VIA GETTY IMAGES

locals hoped to find gold in mountains behind the town. Instead, they made fortunes on the region's towering redwood forests, converting them to lumber for shipment to San Francisco and other important western ports.

How to Get There
The Table Bluff tower stands on Woodley Island in the Eureka Inner Harbor. Follow US 101 into Eureka, turn toward the water on Route 255, and follow signs to the lighthouse. The nearby Humboldt Bay Maritime Museum has the station's fourth-order Fresnel lens on display. For more information visit humboldtbaymaritimemusuem.com or call (707) 444–9440.

Cape Mendocino Light
Capetown, California
1868

California's westernmost point is also one of its most imposing headlands. Cape Mendocino's soaring 1,400-foot cliffs drop almost vertically into the Pacific. Although the cape was among the West's most famous seamarks and most feared navigational obstacles, no light was placed here until the late 1860s.

Establishing a lighthouse on the cape proved a daunting challenge. The first ship bringing supplies to the construction site wrecked on the merciless rocks to the south. When a second ship finally delivered the necessary materials, they had to be hoisted with ropes hundreds of feet up the cliffs. Laborers were forced to endure weeks of rain and fog and to camp out in howling winds. Despite these difficulties, workers eventually completed a two-story brick dwelling and barn and erected a sixteen-sided iron tower that had been prefabricated by machinists in San Francisco. The Cape Mendocino beacon first lit the cape on the night of December 1, 1868.

Focused by a huge first-order Fresnel lens, the beacon had a focal plane more than 400 feet above the Pacific, enabling the light to reach mariners more than 25 miles at sea. After more than a century of service, the powerful Cape Mendocino Light was deactivated during the 1970s. It was replaced by a smaller and less powerful automated light placed higher up on the cliffs. The original lighthouse stood empty for decades. Then, in 1998, its nearly ruined metal tower was moved to Shelter Cove, where it now graces a small park.

How to Get There
Near Garberville on US 101 take the Redway exit and drive west following the signs to Shelter Cove. The Cape Mendocino tower is in Mal Coombs Park off Machi Road. For more information visit capemendicinolighthouse.org.

Punta Gorda Lighthouse
Petrolia, California
1912

A rounded, nearly treeless cape thrusting 800 feet above the sea, Punta Gorda rises above the northern California coast like a fist waiting to smash vessels that venture too close to its jagged rocks. Eight ships were lost near Punta Gorda between 1899 and 1907. The last of these, the *Columbia*, took 87 people down with her. Prompted by these disasters, Congress funded a light station in 1908, but building the new lighthouse proved extremely difficult. Materials had to be landed well to the north of the site and then dragged down the beach on horse-drawn sleds. Nonetheless, by 1912, the tower's fourth-order Fresnel lens began to cast its flashing light over the sea.

Since it was as difficult to maintain as it had been to build, the lighthouse was abandoned by the Coast Guard as soon as it became practical to do so. The station was closed permanently in 1951, and the lighthouse fell into ruin. Most station buildings were burned in the 1970s to keep out squatters. All that remains today is a single-story concrete watch room with a spiral staircase leading to an iron lantern room. Resting on a bluff 48 feet above the surf, the entire structure stands only 27 feet high.

How to Get There
From US 101 in northern California, take the Cape Mendocino Road from Fortuna and follow it to the village of Petrolia. A 3.5-mile trail leads to the lighthouse.

Point Cabrillo Light
Mendocino, California
1909

The sea and land have never been good neighbors at Point Cabrillo. Storm-driven waves often slam against the shore, hurling salt spray onto rocks near the top of 60-foot cliffs. Fog rises off the ocean to blanket the point for as much as 1,000 hours each year. Weather makes this coast perilous for mariners and dreary for lighthouse personnel, but for nearly 65 years keepers and their assistants have lived and worked here full-time.

Since 1909 a small clapboard fog signal building and attached octagonal wooden light tower have guarded this lonely headland and warned mariners to steer clear. The building looks more like a country church or school than a lighthouse, and that seems fitting, for keepers and their families lived a bucolic existence at Point Cabrillo. In addition to maintaining the light, keepers often raised vegetables and looked after cows, pigs, and chickens. This decidedly rural life came to an end in 1973 when the station was automated and the last of the keepers packed up and headed for other, less isolated Coast Guard assignments.

During automation, the station's third-order Fresnel lens gave way to a more easily maintained airport-style beacon. No longer needed, the tower, fog signal building, and other structures fell into disrepair and, in time, might have been demolished had not lighthouse preservationists stepped in to save them. Now fully restored and well maintained, these structures are part of California's Point Cabrillo Light Station State Historic Park. The station's original third-order Fresnel lens has been repaired and returned to the tower where it once more serves mariners.

It is fortunate that anything remained of the lighthouse to be restored. Time and demolition crews were not the station's only enemies. On more than one occasion the Pacific Ocean itself threatened to carry away the lighthouse. In 1960 a gale struck Point Cabrillo with such force that two-ton boulders were thrown up onto the cliffs by waves that rolled over the fields and into the heavy doors on the seaward side of the tower.

How to Get There
A few miles north of Mendocino or south of Fort Bragg, turn off Highway 1 onto Point Cabrillo Road. Take Lighthouse Road to the station. For more information visit point cabrillo.org or call (707) 937–6123. For a romantic overnight stay in the old keeper's house or station cottages call (707) 937–5033.

Point Arena Light
Point Arena, California
1870

Like much of the California coastline, Point Arena turns a hospitable face to those who come by land, but bares its teeth to mariners. Jagged, saw-toothed rocks rise from the waves just offshore and 2.5 miles to the west, predatory Point Arena Rock rises from the sea, waiting to tear open the hulls of ships. Since 1870 the powerful, flashing beacon of the Point Arena Lighthouse has warned vessels of these dangers.

The original station consisted not only of a tower, dwelling, and outbuildings, but also had a pair of 12-inch steam whistles protruding from the roof of a specially built fog-signal building. The steam for the whistles was generated by wood-burning boilers that consumed up to 100 tons of firewood during especially foggy years. Keepers not only had to tend the light and feed the hungry boilers, but also brace themselves against the constant threat of storms and earthquakes.

The point's rugged topography was created by movement of the San Andreas Fault, which lies beneath the lighthouse. The legendary fault slipped and growled in 1906, flattening much of San Francisco and, not surprisingly, devastating the Point Arena light station. Fatally cracked by the earthquake, the original brick tower could not be repaired and had to be torn down and replaced. To buttress the new, 115-foot tower against future quakes, builders reinforced its concrete walls with steel. The first-order Fresnel lens placed here in 1908 remains in the tower, but nowadays the station's powerful flashing beacon is produced by an efficient modern optic located outside the lantern room.

How to Get There

Located about 1 mile north of Point Arena off Lighthouse Road, the lighthouse is open to the public daily. A museum in the old fog signal building recounts the station's history. Lodging is available in the old keeper's house and other station buildings. For more information visit pointarenalighthouse.com or call (877) 725–4448.

Point Reyes Light
Point Reyes National Seashore, California
1870

In 1885, Point Reyes keeper E.G. Chamberlain wrote the following: *Solitude, where are your charms? . . . Better dwell in the midst of alarms than in this horrible place.* It is not hard to understand keeper Chamberlain's melancholy when one considers that Point Reyes is socked in by fog more than 110 days a year. Keepers lived and worked on this isolated and frequently shrouded point of land for more than a century and at times must have thought they were on another world.

Considered one of the West's most dangerous navigational obstacles, Point Reyes sweeps more than 15 miles southwestward from the southeastward-trending northern California coast. With its fog, wind, and tricky currents, the mostly low-lying point has been tearing open the hulls of ships since at least the sixteenth century.

Despite the number of ships that ran aground here, centuries would pass before any determined effort was made to mark this prominent navigational hazard. Point Reyes was so rugged and remote that construction of a lighthouse here was thought impractical if not altogether impossible. After a rash of shipwrecks during and after the California Gold Rush, US maritime officials decided that something had to be done, and in 1870 a lighthouse was finally built at the far seaward end of the point.

Fitted with a first-order Fresnel lens weighing more than two tons, the station warned mariners with an extraordinarily powerful light that could be seen for more than 24 miles. Shining out over the Pacific from an elevation of more than 280 feet, the beacon made navigation of this stretch of the California coast much safer.

Point Reyes was considered an unattractive duty station by most keepers, who found the fog and isolation hard to endure, but some apparently thrived on the seclusion. For instance, Gustav Zetterquist held the job of Point Reyes keeper from 1930 until 1951, a stretch of more than twenty years. The station was finally automated in 1975, much to the relief, no doubt, of some lonely keeper.

Although taken out of service in 1975, the station's huge Fresnel lens still dominates the sixteen-sided brick tower, which despite its lofty elevation, is just shy of 40 feet tall. Maintained nowadays by park rangers at the Point Reyes National Seashore, the lens, with its 16 separate bull's-eyes, fascinates visitors but no longer guides mariners. That task is handled by a modern optic mounted on top of the old fog signal building.

How to Get There

The lighthouse is in Point Reyes National Seashore off Route 1 northwest of San Francisco. Stop first at the Bear Valley Visitor Center near the entrance. A separate Visitor Center is located near the lighthouse where an observation platform provides a fine view of the facility. A seemingly endless flight of 300 steps leads down to the tower, and only visitors in good physical condition should attempt the climb. Keep in mind that the weather at Point Reyes is unpredictable. For additional information call (415) 669–1250.

Point Bonita Light
San Francisco, California
1855

Built in 1855 on a high ledge more than 300 feet above the sea, the original station had a 56-foot brick tower and a detached, Cape Cod–style dwelling. Since it pointed the way to San Francisco, the Point Bonita lighthouse was assigned it a powerful second-order Fresnel lens. The light could be seen from up to 20 miles at sea, except in a heavy fog, which could make it completely invisible.

Since low-lying clouds frequently masked the beacon, the station needed an effective fog signal. At first, the station relied on a surplus army cannon fired off with an earsplitting roar by keepers whenever fog rolled in, which it did nearly every day. The cannon was eventually replaced by a 1,500-pound bell.

In time officials decided to build another lighthouse closer to the water, where its beacon would be more effective. Construction of the new lighthouse got under way in 1872, but fitting it onto the only available site—a frightfully narrow ledge about 120 feet above the waves—was no simple matter. To bring materials to the site, a landing platform, derrick, and incline railway had to be built, and a tunnel blasted through more than 100 feet of solid rock. It took more than five years to complete the 33-foot tower and associated structures. Equipped with the Fresnel lens from the original lighthouse and a pair of steam-driven fog sirens, the station was, at last, ready for service by the winter of 1877.

Point Bonita. MICHAEL MARFELL/MOMENT VIA GETTY IMAGES

Like all California structures, the Point Bonita Lighthouse had to withstand potentially devastating natural forces. The tower survived the earthquake that leveled much of San Francisco in 1906. During the 1940s, however, a landslide destroyed the land bridge that connected the tower and fog signal building. The Coast Guard first replaced it with a wooden bridge, then with the attractive suspension bridge that still serves the station today. In 1981 the Point Bonita Light became the last of California's lighthouses to be automated.

How to Get There

This extraordinarily scenic lighthouse located off Highway 101 just north of San Francisco is now part of the Golden Gate National Recreation Area. From San Francisco cross the Golden Gate Bridge, take the Alexander Avenue exit, and follow Conzelman Road to the lighthouse. The winding roadway provides spectacular views of the city and the coast. Sensible shoes are recommended since reaching the lighthouse requires a hike of more than a mile. For more information visit nps.gov/goga or call (415) 561–4700.

East Brother Light
Richmond, California
1874

Built in 1874, the classically Victorian East Brother Lighthouse now serves as both a navigational light guiding vessels into San Pablo Bay and as a popular bed-and-breakfast inn. Located on a small island just off San Pablo Point, the lighthouse marks the channel through the narrow and often treacherous San Pablo Straits that links the Sacramento River estuary to the open San Francisco Bay.

Unable to buy property on the mainland at an acceptable price, the government resorted to building the station on tiny East Brother Island. Construction crews had to blast away much of the one-third acre island to level the site. There was hardly room on what remained to squeeze the combination two-story tower and dwelling and separate fog signal building. In 1967 the Coast Guard decided to automate the station, place its light on a pole, and tear down the old buildings. Local preservationists managed to save the structure and, over time, restore the station to its original Victorian charm. The fifth-order light is still in operation.

How to Get There
For overnight reservations at the East Brother Light Station visit ebls.org or call (510) 233–2385. Day visits are also encouraged.

Yerba Buena Light
San Francisco, California
1874

This light once guided dozens of passenger ferries passing back and forth each day between San Francisco and Oakland. For many years the U.S. Lighthouse Service maintained a major depot on the island for storage of buoys, lenses, lamp oil, and other supplies and equipment. Since 1939, San Francisco's magnificent Bay Bridge has carried most cross-bay traffic, but the light on Yerba Buena Island still shines. Nowadays, it mostly serves pleasure craft and the Coast Guard base, which takes up the entire 140-acre island. A Coast Guard admiral lives in the old keeper's dwelling. The

original fifth-order Fresnel lens still crowns the station's two-story octagonal tower and displays an occulting white light.

How to Get There
Located on an active Coast Guard station, the lighthouse is not open to the public. Its light can be seen from the bay and from a variety of points along the shore. The lighthouse itself can be seen from the Bay Bridge, which links San Francisco to Oakland.

Alcatraz Island Light
San Francisco, California
1854

Derived from *alcatraces*—the Spanish word for *pelican*—the name Alcatraz now has a cold and forbidding ring to it, and no wonder. For years Alcatraz Island in San Francisco Bay was the home of Al Capone and many other notorious criminals. Here they served hard time at a federal penitentiary made escape-proof by high concrete walls and the shark-infested waters of the bay.

In contrast mariners and lighthouse lovers have warm feelings the island since it is the source of one of the most famous and romantic navigational beacons in the whole world. Nearly 170 years ago, Francis Gibbons built the island's original lighthouse, a Cape Cod–style dwelling with a short tower peeking just above its roof. The lamps inside its third-order Fresnel lens were first lit on the evening of June 1, 1854. At that time gold-hungry miners were still arriving in their thousands by sea, and the Alcatraz Island beacon guided them into San Francisco Bay and on toward their respective destinies.

The great San Francisco earthquake of 1906 caused Alcatraz keeper B. F. Leeds to believe he was witnessing the *end of the world*, but not so. However, the shaking did end the career of the little Gibbons lighthouse. The severely damaged building could not be repaired and, in 1909, was replaced by an 84-foot, reinforced concrete tower with adjacent bay-style dwelling. The height of the octagonal tower allowed its light to be seen above the high walls of the military prison then under construction on the island.

For more than fifty years, the light station would share its rugged roost with prisons, both military and civilian. The infamous federal "pen" accepted its first prisoners in 1934. As a result, keepers here endured many sleepless days and nights during major breakouts and riots. The worst incident came in 1946 when inmates took over the prison, holding police and a contingent of U.S. Marines at bay for nearly two

days. Both the lighthouse and its keeper survived the uprising. The light was automated in 1963, not long before the doors of the prison slammed shut for the last time. Ironically, the two-story lighthouse keeper's residence, having survived both sea storms and prison riots, was badly burned during a protracted demonstration by young Native Americans in 1969.

How to Get There

Alcatraz Island is part of the Golden Gate National Recreation Area and can be reached via a variety of tour options from San Francisco. For more information visit nps.gov/goga or call (415) 561–4700. Tour boats leave for Alcatraz Island several times a day from Pier 41 in the city's Fisherman's Wharf District.

Fort Point Lighthouse
San Francisco, California
1855

Completed in 1853, at about the same time as the original Alcatraz Island lighthouse, the Fort Point Lighthouse had an important job to do, that of marking the channel through the Golden Gate and into San Francisco Bay. Yet the lighthouse stood empty for more than a year while waiting for its third-order Fresnel lens to arrive from France. The lens though, was never installed and the tower's lamps never lit. Before the station could be placed in operation, the lighthouse was torn down to make way for the massive brick walls of Fort Winfield Scott. The Fresnel lens originally intended for Fort Point was shipped south for use in the Point Pinos Lighthouse on Monterey Bay, where it still shines today after more than 170 years.

While the three-story fortress was under construction, workers built a wooden light tower at the water's edge. By 1864 storm-driven Pacific waves threatened to sweep the tower away and undermine the foundations of the fort. To make way for a protective seawall, the lighthouse was torn down again. This time it was replaced by a 27-foot iron-skeleton tower perched like a giant seabird atop the fort's lofty parapet. The additional height made the light, focused by a rather modest fifth-order lens, easier for approaching seamen to see.

The station served its purpose for more than seven decades, until construction of the Golden Gate Bridge made it obsolete. The station's light was snuffed out for good in 1934. Towering 740 feet above the sea, the bridge itself is a mammoth lighthouse. From miles away mariners can see its lights and recognize the distinctive inverted arches of its supporting cables. Completed and opened to traffic in 1937, the bridge is one of the world's most recognizable structures.

How to Get There
Approaching the Golden Gate Bridge from the south on US 101, take the last San Francisco exit, then follow Lincoln Boulevard and Long Avenue to Fort Point National Historical Site. For more information visit nps.gov/goga or call (415) 561–4700. Open daily except for major holidays, the old fort with its tiny lighthouse offers wonderful views of San Francisco and the Golden Gate Bridge.

Farallon Islands Light
South Farallon Island, California
1855

During the 1850s, when the US government shouldered the daunting task of lighting the nation's West Coast, maritime officials decided to start with the most strategic and dangerous locations. Counted among these were the nearly barren Farallon Islands, about 20 miles west of San Francisco. Rising unexpectedly from the Pacific, these rugged, wave-bound rocks had brought more than a few vessels to grief. Government maritime officials reasoned that a powerful beacon here would not only warn mariners but also point the way to the Golden Gate and the safe waters of San Francisco Bay.

Built in 1853 by a construction crew consisting of failed Gold Rush prospectors and a mule named "Paddy," the lighthouse was never used. Like several other early California lighthouses, it proved too small to serve its purpose. When the station's first-order Fresnel lens arrived by ship from France, the bulky bronze and glass optic could not be squeezed into the narrow tower. As a result, the original structure had to be torn down and rebuilt. The new, larger tower was not completed until late in 1854. Finally, on January 1, 1855, the station's lamps were lit, and its powerful light began to shine out over the Pacific.

Early keepers at this station were caught in the middle of a bizarre "egg war." Poachers made large profits stealing eggs from the millions of seabirds nesting on South Farallon and other nearby islands. So large and lucrative were their hauls that greedy poachers fought with one another for gathering rights. When gunfire erupted, California lawmen stepped in and drove off the poachers.

One of the nation's most isolated lighthouses, the Farallon Islands station was automated in 1972. At the same time, the big, first-order Fresnel was exchanged for a modern optic.

How to Get There

The various seabird species that once provided eggs for gold rush breakfasts now find safe haven in the Farallon National Wildlife Refuge. These protected islands are difficult to reach, but the Oceanic Society in San Francisco offers cruises that provide views of the lighthouse as well as the islands' abundant wildlife; for more information visit oceanicsociety.org or call (415) 256–9604. The original Farallon first-order lens is now on display at the San Francisco Maritime National Historical Park near Fisherman's Wharf; call (415) 561–7000.

Point Montara Light
Montara, California
1900

In 1868, the steamer *Colorado* ran aground on a ledge near Point Montara. Four years later the freighter *Acuelo* wrecked just below the point, spilling into the sea a cargo of coal and iron worth at least $150,000. The latter disaster led to the placement of a fog signal on Point Montara in 1872, but many years would pass before the Point Montara fog-signal station became a full-fledged lighthouse.

A simple pole light, set up in 1900, served until 1912, when it was replaced by a wooden tower. The existing 30-foot cast-iron tower was built at the edge of the rocky point in 1928. Its light still shines out toward the Pacific from an elevation of 70 feet. The station's fourth-order Fresnel lens gave way to a modern optic in 1970.

Iron light towers like the one that now marks Point Montara were developed during the mid-nineteenth century for use at navigational stations where they would likely be exposed to harsh weather conditions. Easily moved, these adaptable structures were often built at foundries and shipped to their assigned locations, or they could be assembled on-site by bolting together curved iron plates, as was the case at Point Montara.

How to Get There
The lighthouse is located off Highway 1 about 25 miles south of San Francisco. Most of the station buildings, including the Victorian-style keeper's quarters, are now used as a youth hostel. For more information check visithalfmoonbay.com or call (650) 728–7177. Visitors are welcome to walk the grounds.

Pigeon Point Light
Pescadero, California
1872

The Pigeon Point Light, some 50 miles south of San Francisco, shines out toward the Pacific from an elevation of more than 150 feet. Less than 40 feet of that height is provided by the point; the rest comes from the 115-foot brick tower. One of the tallest light towers on the Pacific Coast, it was built in 1872 with brick shipped from the East all the way around Cape Horn. The land, lighthouse, and huge first-order Fresnel lens cost the government approximately $20,000. While the big, polished-glass prismatic lens remains in the tower, a modern optic mounted on the gallery rail now focuses the powerful Pigeon Point beacon. Pigeon Point takes its name from the Yankee clipper *Carrier Pigeon*, wrecked here in 1853.

How to Get There

Now open to the public as a hostelry, the station is located just off Highway 1 south of the small, bucolic town of Pescadero. The grounds are open year-round. For more information visit parks.ca.gov/pigeonpoint or call (650) 879–0633.

Part Four

ROMANTIC BEACONS OF THE GOLDEN SHORES

Central and Southern California

For travelers who love beautiful scenery, the Central and Southern Coasts of California comprise an earthly paradise. Various irresistible natural forces have conspired to make it so, for here a bold range of geologically young mountains meets the planet's oldest and most extensive ocean. Whether seen from land or water, this coast is enchanting, but mariners know it is not just a place of beauty. Mortal danger lurks along these shores, and sailors have known this for hundreds of years.

Colonial-era Spanish treasure ships, bearing silk and spices from the Orient, spent months crossing thousands of miles of trackless, storm-lashed to reach California, but were seldom so threatened as when they approached the coast. Just as they are today, California's headlands were frequently draped in fog and all but invisible. A captain's first warning of landfall might be the grinding and splintering of his hull on stone. Or a storm might blow up suddenly and send his ship hurtling out of control toward the rocks.

Many of the ships and crews lost along the California coast simply vanished, never to be seen or heard from again. No one knows how many wrecked ships may lie in the waters off California. The carnage along these shores has continued right up into our own times. Even with coastal lights, the best charts, and the finest navigational instruments to guide them, mariners still get lost here—with disastrous results.

Ghost Fleet

Perhaps the worst maritime disaster in California history took place on September 8, 1923, when a fleet of fourteen U.S. Navy destroyers took a wrong turn off Point Arguello. Pushing south from San Francisco to San Diego, the fleet was under the overall command of Captain Edward Watson, who ordered his ships to maintain a precise military formation, running one behind the other about two minutes apart. Despite a thick fog cloaking both the sea and the shoreline just to the east, the fleet was making good time, steaming steadily ahead at twenty knots.

To maintain a uniform distance from the shore, Captain Watson intended to turn his vessels to the east once they had passed Point Conception, where the California coastline changes course. This shift in the shoreline is marked by a pair of lights, one on Point Arguello and the other a few dozen miles southeast on Point Conception. Peering into the darkness, Captain Watson had seen neither of these two critical beacons. Growing impatient, he became convinced that he had missed the lights in the heavy fog and that the flotilla was now well to the south of Point Conception.

Just as he was about to give the order that would turn his destroyers eastward, supposedly into the Santa Barbara Channel, Watson received a surprising message from the *Delphy*, the fleet's lead vessel. The *Delphy's* navigator reported receiving the signal of the radio beacon on Point Arguello. The flotilla commander was momentarily puzzled. If the report were accurate and the signal was the one from Point Arguello, then the *Delphy* and the rest of the fleet were still well to the north of Point Conception. The captain decided his navigator must be mistaken. For one thing, he had received a second radio signal that seemed to indicate the destroyers had cleared Conception. For another, Captain Watson was an old sailor who trusted his instinct for dead reckoning more than any navigational contraption. He gave the order.

Unfortunately, the second signal had been false, and the captain's reckoning was mistaken. Shortly after the ships began their turn to the east, chaos broke out at a place called Honda, a mile or so north of the Point Arguello Lighthouse. Metal screamed and ruptured boilers hissed as the *Delphy* and, one after another, the *Lee*, *Young*, *Woodbury*, *Chauncey*, *Nicholas*, and *Fuller* slammed into the shore, striking the rocks at approximately two-minute intervals.

Point Arguello Lighthouse keepers Gotford Olson, Arvel Settles, and Jesse Mygrants could hear the drumming of engines as the destroyers steamed toward their doom. Fearing the worst, they hurried down to water's edge, where they were confronted by a disaster of overwhelming proportions: an entire fleet of Navy ships run aground. The keepers immediately pitched in to help, pulling dozens and then hundreds of shipwrecked sailors out of the surf. Injured men were carried to the lighthouse for treatment. Later, the keepers would receive commendations for their bravery and determination to save lives.

In all, seven ships went aground that night. Another seven managed to turn away in time to reach safe waters. Twenty-three sailors lost their lives and many others were injured. In memory of the ships and men lost in this tragic mishap, a memorial anchor was placed at Honda on a bluff overlooking the site of the wrecks.

Countless vessels and the mariners aboard them owe an incalculable debt to the long line of lighthouses strung out along the California coast. In fact, so do the rest of us, because neither the West nor the nation as a whole could have prospered without them. California's lighthouses still have much to offer for those who approach them from the landward side as well. This is especially true along the Central and Southern coasts, where many historic lights are open to the public and visitors may celebrate the lives and exploits of keepers both alive and dead.

Ghost Lights

It should come as no surprise that lighthouses seem to be prime real estate for ghosts. That may be true in part because so many lighthouses—western ones in particular— are Victorian in style, giving them just the sort of look we often associate with the spectral and with things that go bump in the night. And because of their exposed locations, lighthouses certainly have more than their share of dark and stormy weather. Whether Victorian or not, the old, abandoned dwellings and tall towers, with their glowing lights, do have a distinctly ghostly feeling about them. Most are, in fact, quite old—a century or more—and have seen many generations of keepers. When stories are told about the keepers and the families who served at these isolated stations years ago, it is easy to imagine their spirits returning to haunt the places where they lived and worked for so long.

More than a few keepers of the Point Vicente Lighthouse have felt a chill run up and down their spines at night—especially when the station's ladylike ghost puts in an appearance. As with most lighthouse ghosts, this one is associated with a tragic story: According to legend, the lady's lover had drowned in a shipwreck, and she walked the grounds of the light station incessantly, waiting for him to rejoin her. For decades, it seemed, the faithful lady drifted over the station grounds, sometimes almost nightly. Keepers and visitors would look out across the station property and there she would be, an indistinct shape floating just above the ground. Some said she wore a flowing white gown.

The mystery of these sightings was eventually solved by a young assistant keeper with an exceptionally quick and skeptical mind. He took careful note of the lady's habits. She appeared only at night and most often when the station's powerful rotating beacon moved in her direction. She had a particular fondness for nights when there

was a light fog. The amateur detective concluded that the feminine ghost was the work of slight imperfections in the third-order Fresnel lens in the lantern room atop the 67-foot tower. As the lens rotated, it refracted light toward the ground in a confusion of arcs. If the refractions came together in just the right way and found a patch of fog, the "lady" appeared. Despite the sensibleness of this explanation, most visitors prefer to believe a ghostly lady still walks the station grounds. And perhaps she does.

Some lighthouses are themselves ghosts. After serving faithfully for decades—sometimes a century or more—they were abandoned and allowed to fall into disrepair and ruin. Other outmoded or no-longer-needed lighthouses were intentionally razed to make room for new government structures. Still others were sold as surplus property to private enterprises for use as yacht clubs, restaurants, or storage houses. California has more than its share of "ghost" lighthouses—historic structures that now exist only in memory. However, the Golden State remains bright with light towers and beacons that still guide mariners. Most, if not all, are well worth a visit. The lights of Central and Southern California are among the most traveler-friendly on the planet.

Santa Cruz Light
Santa Cruz, California
1869

The Santa Cruz Lighthouse was built in 1869 to guide lumber and lime freighters in and out of the bustling harbor of this charming Central California city. Laura Heacox, daughter of the station's first keeper, tended the light for nearly half a century. Its beacon darkened during World War II to prevent attack from the sea, the wood and brick lighthouse was torn down in 1948. The brick light tower seen here today is not the original but rather was built in 1967 with private funds as a memorial to Mark Abbott, a teenage surfing enthusiast who drowned in a nearby accident. Although the navigational light is an active aide to navigation, the interior of the building serves as a surfing museum.

How to Get There
Follow West Cliff Drive in Santa Cruz to Lighthouse Point. The museum is free and open every afternoon except Tuesday. For more information visit cityofsantacruz.com or call (831) 420–5270.

Point Pinos Light
Pacific Grove, California
1855

Now surrounded by a lush golf course, the West Coast's oldest active lighthouse is leased by the Coast Guard to the Pacific Grove Museum of Natural History, which uses it as a maritime museum. Like many other early California lighthouses built during the 1850s by contractor Francis Gibbons, this one consists of a Cape Cod–style, stone keeper's residence with a conical brick tower rising through its roof. Originally granite, the structure was covered over with reinforced concrete following the severe earthquake that devastated San Francisco and much of the central California coast in 1906. The third-order Fresnel lens in place here since 1855 still shines.

Counted among the West's historic treasures, the old lighthouse has played host to many notables such as John Steinbeck and Robert Louis Stevenson. The station's first keeper, former gold rush miner Charles Layton, died in a shoot-out with the notorious bandito Anastasio Garcia. Layton's wife then took over as keeper.

How to Get There
Located on Lighthouse Avenue between Sunset Drive and Asilomar Avenue at the far western end of Pacific Grove, the lighthouse is open to the public on Saturday and Sunday afternoons. For more information visit pointpinoslighthouse.org or call (831) 648–5722.

Point Sur Light
Big Sur, California
Established: 1889

At Big Sur the churning Pacific makes relentless war on a chain of coastal mountains. The same natural forces—weather and geology—responsible for this scenic spectacle have also made it a very dangerous place for ships. Countless seafaring vessels—and one dirigible—have been lost here. But since 1889, the powerful beacon of the Point Sur Lighthouse has warned mariners to keep away.

It was once thought impossible to build a light station on Big Sur's precipitous cliffs, but the U.S. Lighthouse Service took up the challenge during the late 1880s. Before construction could begin, workers had to lay tracks for a special railroad car to carry materials and supplies to the rugged sandstone mountain known as Point Sur. The project took two years of hard work and more than $100,000 to complete. Finally ready for service in 1889, the station consisted of a forty-foot-tall granite tower atop the cliffs and a collection of dwellings and other buildings down nearer the water.

Keepers found the lighthouse almost as hard to maintain as it had been to build. Every night they had to trudge up the 395 steps leading to the tower to tend the light. The Point Sur Light was finally automated in 1972, all but eliminating the need for the long daily climb. At that time a rotating aero-beacon replaced the original first-order Fresnel lens.

How to Get There
The lighthouse can be seen from several places along Highway 1 on the way from Monterey to Big Sur. A turnout near the crest of lofty Hurricane Ridge, about 15 miles south of Carmel, provides a clear, though distant, view of the lighthouse. The station's enormous first-order Fresnel lens is now impressively displayed at the Monterey Maritime Museum near Fisherman's Wharf in Monterey. For more information visit monteryhistory.org or call (831) 372–2608.

Piedras Blancas Light
San Simeon, California
1875

Automation transformed this once handsome lighthouse into an ugly duckling. During a 1949 renovation, its lovely old lantern was lopped off and a rotating, airport-style beacon was set atop the decapitated tower to do the work of the original first-order Fresnel lens.

When completed in 1875, the cone-shaped brick tower soared 90 feet above a grassy knoll that boosted its overall height to more than 140 feet. With its ornate gallery and crown-like lantern, the tower looked a bit like a giant, elegantly carved, ivory chess rook. The much less attractive modern beacon that serves here today is no less powerful as it can be seen from up to 21 miles out in the Pacific.

Despite its appearance, the lighthouse is a favorite of tourists who visit the area to see the Hearst Castle in San Simeon or to view the impressive colony of elephant seals that wallow on the beaches near the tower. These jumbo seals are so big that when lying partially buried in the sand, they can be mistaken for large boulders.

How to Get There

The lighthouse is located on Highway 1 about 1 mile north of San Simeon. Although closed to the public, the tower can be viewed from the roadside. The elephant seals can be viewed from a large parking area not far from the lighthouse. (For obvious reasons, these jumbo-sized seals can be quite dangerous, and visitors are not allowed on the beach.) The original Piedras Blancas first-order lens is housed in a modest lantern-like structure on Main Street in the nearby town of Cambria. For more information on the lighthouse visit piedrasblancas.org.

Point San Luis Lighthouse
Avila Beach, California
1890

Although the lovely, old Spanish town of San Luis Obispo had one of the best harbors in southern California, it was among the last West Coast ports to receive a lighthouse. Regional political squabbling blocked congressional appropriations until the late 1880s, when funds finally became available.

Built on an isolated point on the west side of San Luis Obispo Bay, the station was ready for service by June 1890. It consisted of a distinctly Victorian two-story residence with a square, 40-foot tower rising from one corner, and a fog signal building with a 10-inch steam whistle. A fourth-order Fresnel lens produced the beacon, which had a focal plane 116 feet above sea level. Because there was no road leading to the point—there still is not—U.S. Lighthouse Service supply steamers made regular calls at the Point San Luis station.

The light was automated in 1974, and about a year later the old lighthouse lost its job to a cylindrical structure built just to the east. The new, far less scenic tower boasts a powerful, modern optic producing a flashing white signal that can be seen from 20 miles at sea.

The Point San Luis Lighthouse was the last of a series of combination light towers and dwellings built in a distinctly Victorian style by the old U.S. Lighthouse Service. Earlier California lighthouses at Ballast Point near San Diego, Point Fermin near Los Angeles, Point Hueneme near Oxnard, and on East Brother Island in San Francisco Bay were built using a similar set of plans. Of these, only the lighthouses at Point Fermin and East Brother Island still stand.

How to Get There

Located in Avila Beach near the university town of San Luis Obispo and the Diablo Canyon Nuclear Power Plant, the lighthouse is open to visitors via trolley tour. The Fresnel lens that served the station for so long is now on display at the lighthouse. For more information visit pointsanluislighthouse.org.

Point Conception Light
Point Conception, California
1856

At Point Conception, ships headed along the California coast must change course, either northward toward San Francisco or eastward toward Los Angeles. Here colliding ocean currents generate some of the worst weather in America, causing experienced seamen to compare Point Conception to South America's notoriously stormy Cape Horn. And well they should. The crushed hulls of wrecked vessels—eighteenth-century Spanish sailing ships and more recent American steamers—litter the churning waters off this dramatic angle of land.

Aware of Point Conception's importance and nightmarish reputation, the US government chose its isolated cliff tops as the site for one of the West's earliest light stations. Built with great difficulty in 1854, the lighthouse was beset with problems from the start. Workmanship of the brick-and-mortar structure was shoddy, and the combination tower and dwelling began to fall apart almost as soon as it was finished. Worse, the tower was too small for the first-order Fresnel lens assigned to it. Finally,

the contractors had to tear the whole thing down and start over again. Then, when the keepers installed the big lens, they discovered that several key parts of the lighting apparatus were missing, and new ones had to be ordered from France.

Once the station finally became operational in 1856, it quickly became apparent that the tower had been built too high on the cliffs. Fog and low-lying clouds frequently obscured the light. Weakened by repeated gales and earthquakes, the building was finally abandoned in 1882 in favor of a better-constructed lighthouse built at a more practical elevation of about 130 feet. The two-foot-thick, 52-foot-high brick and granite walls have aged well. The lighthouse remains as solid as ever, and the station's original 10-foot-high, first-order lens remains in place. Nowadays, however, the Point Conception beacon is produced by a modern optic mounted on the railing of the lantern gallery.

How to Get There
Very difficult, if not impossible, to approach from land or sea, the station is closed to the public.

Santa Barbara Light
Santa Barbara, California
1856

A simple, white tower on a Coast Guard base just west of Santa Barbara now serves in place of the city's historic lighthouse, destroyed during a major earthquake in 1925. Among the first lighthouses in the West, the original structure was built by contractor George Nagle for a modest $8,000. Like many early California lighthouses, it consisted of a Cape Cod–style dwelling with a tower rising through its roof. For many years the original lighthouse was the home of Julia Williams, one of America's most famous lighthouse keepers. She tended the Santa Barbara Light for more than forty years, and it is said she spent only two nights away from the station during that time.

How to Get There
The existing automated light tower is closed to the public. However, the flashing beacon can be seen from the water and a number of points along the shore.

Anacapa Island Light
Anacapa Island
1912

From a distance Southern California's beautiful Channel Islands seem placid, but their jagged rocks have torn apart countless ships. The Spanish treasure ship *San Sebastion* wrecked here in 1784, dumping its shipment of gold doubloons into the surf. In 1853 the steamer *Winfield Scott* slammed into Anacapa Island, stranding 250 passengers for several weeks without food or shelter.

Government officials had long recognized the need for a light to warn mariners of the dangers here, but until the twentieth century, few believed a lighthouse could be built on the island's rugged, almost perpendicular, cliffs. In 1912 the project was finally attempted, and after considerable effort, a light station was established on Anacapa Island. Equipped with an automated, acetylene lamp, its iron-skeleton tower stood near the spot where the *Winfield Scott* had run onto the rocks nearly 60 years earlier.

In 1932, the Lighthouse Service assigned resident keepers to the station and built a new, 55-foot-tall masonry tower. Although not as tall, the tower looks much like the one at Point Vicente near Los Angeles. The height of the cliffs placed its light 277 feet above the ocean, from which elevation its third-order beacon could be seen from 20 miles away. Always difficult to supply, especially with fresh water, the station was automated in 1969. A modern lens replaced the original Fresnel in 1991. The original lens is on display at the Anacapa Island Visitor Center.

How to Get There

The Anacapa Lighthouse is now part of Channel Islands National Park, one of the nation's foremost scenic wonders. For more information visit nps.gov/chis or call (805) 658–5730. To reach the park's main visitor center from US 101 in Ventura, follow Victoria Avenue, Olivas Park Drive, and Spinnaker Drive to Ventura Harbor. Visits to Anacapa and other islands are available through park concessionaires in Ventura; visit islandpackers.com or call (805) 642–1393.

Point Vicente Light
Los Angeles, California
1926

Situated on a cliff high above the blue Pacific and surrounded by graceful palms, the sparkling white Point Vicente tower fits everyone's romantic image of a Southern California lighthouse. In fact, film crews have used it as the backdrop for countless movie and television scenes. Built in 1926 near the edge of a rocky cliff more than a hundred feet above the ocean, the 67-foot cylindrical tower is crowned by a handsome lantern with cross-hatched windows. The original third-order Fresnel lens still shines each night, producing a powerful 1.1 million candlepower flash every twenty seconds. It can be seen from 24 miles away.

Naturally, this quintessential lighthouse has a resident ghost. The ladylike phantom appears only on foggy nights and is said to be the former lover of a sailor who died in a shipwreck on Point Vicente. Skeptics say she is nothing more than an optical illusion created by stray refractions of the station's lens, but that should not deter romantic souls from enjoying the legend and perhaps casting an eye about when fog rolls across the point.

Perhaps Point Vicente's feminine ghost took a holiday during World War II. While fighting in the Pacific raged, the station's Fresnel was blacked out to prevent Japanese submarines from using it to help them track down vulnerable American freighters. A smaller, less brilliant light served Point Vicente until the war was over, at which time the original Fresnel lens was once more placed in service. Incidentally, the Point Vicente's lens is considerably older than the lighthouse itself. The lens had been used in an Alaska lighthouse for nearly forty years before being brought to California in 1926.

How to Get There

The lighthouse is located north of Marineland off Palos Verdes Drive. A fine view of the light can be had from the grounds of the nearby Point Vicente Interpretive Center. Exhibits recount the history of the lighthouse and explore the natural history of the Palos Verdes peninsula. For more information visit rpvca.gov.

Point Fermin Lighthouse
Los Angeles, California
1874

No longer in operation, the Point Fermin Lighthouse remains a venerable landmark. Built in 1874 with highly durable redwood, its Victorian-era Italianate styling and decorative gingerbread make it an architectural delight. Rising through the middle of the pitched roof, a square tower supports a lantern so small it almost goes unnoticed.

One might think this unusual structure unique, but not so. To cut costs, government engineers often used the same general set of plans to build more than one lighthouse, as was the case with the

Point Fermin and its sister lighthouse at Point Hueneme near Oxnard. Unfortunately, the original Point Hueneme Lighthouse was torn down at the beginning of World War II, but in addition to the one on Point Fermin, two very similar buildings remain standing at the East Brother Island Light Station in San Francisco Bay and at Hereford Inlet in New Jersey. Not coincidentally, all four of these lighthouses were completed in 1874.

If not for the efforts of a small group of history-minded preservationists, the Point Fermin Lighthouse might have suffered the same fate as its twin at Point Hueneme. The fourth-order Fresnel lens that once shone here was removed during World War II when the structure was pressed into service as a coastal watchtower. During the decades that followed, the station's lantern was removed and the building itself fell into such disrepair that the government planned to demolish it. But local lighthouse lovers stepped in to save the old lighthouse. Its lantern replaced, the old lighthouse now graces Point Fermin City Park.

How to Get There
Now maintained as a museum by the City of Los Angeles, the lighthouse is open to the public on most afternoons. To reach Point Fermin City Park and the lighthouse follow Route 110 to Gaffney Street and turn north. The lighthouse stands on Paseo Del Mar west of Pacific Avenue. The park offers an excellent place to view the Los Angeles Harbor Light, as well. For more information visit pflhs.org.

Los Angeles Harbor Light
Los Angeles, California
1913

Rising more than 70 feet above the Pacific, the Romanesque Los Angeles Harbor Lighthouse has anchored the far end of the San Pedro Harbor Breakwater for more than a century. Despite gales, earthquakes, and even a brush with a U.S. Navy battleship, the old tower has remained solid and functional since its construction in 1913. Its distinctive vertical black stripes and flashing emerald-green light are familiar sights to sailors entering the harbor and boaters enjoying the waters off Los Angeles.

Keepers lived here full time until the station was automated in 1973. The Coast Guard replaced the original fourth-order Fresnel lens with a modern optic when the facility was converted to solar power during the 1980s. The Los Angeles Maritime Museum in San Pedro now proudly displays the original 3,000-pound classic lens.

How to Get There
Somewhat resembling a column from an ancient temple, the Los Angeles Harbor Lighthouse is best seen from the deck of a boat or ferry. The tower can also be seen from Pacific Avenue and from Point Fermin City Park, where visitors can also enjoy the Point Fermin Lighthouse. Located nearby at the lower end of Sixth Street in San Pedro, the Los Angeles Maritime Museum features informative lighthouse exhibits. For more information visit lamaritimemuseum.org or call (310) 548–7618.

Old Point Loma Light
San Diego, California
1855

Visitors to the Cabrillo National Monument near San Diego have a real treat in store: a chance to tour the West's oldest still-standing lighthouse. Although the Old Point Loma lantern has been dark for more than a century, the building remains in excellent condition and looks much the way it did when it first brightened the Southern California

coast during the 1850s. The old station provides a link to California's storied past and to the earliest efforts to light America's Pacific seaboard.

According to legend, Point Loma was named for a Russian girl who survived a shipwreck on these rugged shores only to be murdered later by an amorous local man whose attentions she had spurned. While this tragic tale has its attractions, the name probably derives from the Portuguese word for "light." It is believed that hundreds of years ago, when California was still part of Spain's colonial empire, soldiers banked fires on lofty Point Loma to help royal supply ships reach harbor safely. Following acquisition of California by the United States in 1848, the government selected this same dramatic headland as the likeliest site for a lighthouse to mark the way to San Diego.

Francis Gibbons, who built many of the West's earliest lighthouses, brought his crew of masons and laborers here during spring 1854 but the work on the lighthouse was not completed until late the following year. Built of locally quarried sandstone and brick brought by ship from Monterey, the combination Cape Cod–style dwelling and 46-foot tower ended up costing Uncle Sam a whopping $30,000. Despite what seemed a hefty price at the time, the structure was not constructed according to specifications. When its first-order Fresnel lens arrived by sailing ship from France, workers could not fit it into the narrow lantern at the top of the tower. Instead, they substituted a third-order lens.

Worse problems lay ahead for the lighthouse. Although the station's third-order lens was less powerful than the one intended for it, the 462-foot elevation of the light made it visible from a distance of over 40 miles. That same extraordinary elevation, however, all too often placed the beacon above the low-lying clouds and fog banks that often enveloped the point. Mariners on the decks of ships below the clouds and fog could barely see the light if, indeed, they could see it at all. So, in 1891, some 36 years after its lamps were first lit, the Old Point Loma Light was deactivated, and a skeleton tower built at a lower, more practical, elevation took its place.

How to Get There

From Interstate 5 in San Diego, follow Catalina Boulevard (Route 209) to Cabrillo Memorial Drive through Fort Rosecrans National Cemetery to Cabrillo National Monument. Having refitted the light with a classical lens and furnished the dwelling much as it might have looked when its first keepers lived there, the Park Service maintains the Old Point Loma Light as a museum. For monument hours and other information visit nps.gov/cabr or call (619) 523–4285.

New Point Loma Light
San Diego, California
1891

Since fog often obscured the original Point Loma beacon, government maritime officials decided to build a second lighthouse here at a lower, more practical elevation. Completed in 1891, the new Point Loma Light consists of a 70-foot, iron-skeleton tower and a separate two-story keeper's residence. A white cylinder centered between the tower's braced iron legs allows access to the lantern room. The original third-order Fresnel lens placed here in 1891 focused the light until 2002 when it was replaced by a modern optic. A horn at the base of the tower alerts vessels when fog shrouds the point.

Iron-skeleton towers like this one are rare on the West Coast of the United States. The technology for building them was developed in the eastern United States during the mid-nineteenth century. With their open-sided walls and stout iron bracing, these towers were designed to withstand extreme weather conditions, especially storm winds and high water.

How to Get There
From Interstate 5 in San Diego, follow Catalina Boulevard (Route 209) to Cabrillo Memorial Drive through to Cabrillo National Monument. Located on an active Coast Guard installation, the station is closed to the public, but can be enjoyed from the monument parking area and from the road leading to the popular tidal pools. The monument has on display the third-order Fresnel lens that produced the Point Loma Lighthouse beacon until 2002. For monument hours and other information visit nps .gov/cabr or call (619) 523–4285.

Index

About the Author

Ray Jones is a writer and publishing consultant living in Pebble Beach, California. Author of more than fifty books, Ray began his writing career as a reporter for weekly newspapers in Texas. He has served as a senior editor and writing coach at *Southern Living* magazine, an editor for Time-Life Books, founding editor of *Albuquerque Living* magazine, and founder and publisher of Country Roads Press. Ray grew up in Macon, Georgia, where he was inspired by the writing of Ernest Hemingway and William Faulkner, and worked his way through college as a disc jockey.